A
Million
Reasons
Why
You
Can't

A Million Reasons Why You Can't*

KATRINA
BUSSELLE,
MACR

*and choosing to do it anyway!

Published by Katrina Busselle LLC
katrina@katrinabusselle.com
katrinabusselle.com
Cold Spring, NY

Katrina Busselle LLC books are available at special quantity
discounts for bulk purchase for sales promotions, premiums,
fundraising, and educational needs. Special books or book excerpts
also can be created to fit specific needs. For details and permission
requests, write to the email address above.

Neither the author nor the publisher shall be liable or responsible
for any loss or damage allegedly arising from any information or
suggestion in this book.

ISBN 979-8-9906804-0-1 (eBook)
ISBN 979-8-9906804-1-8 (paperback)
ISBN 979-8-9906804-2-5 (hardback)
ISBN 979-8-9906804-3-2 (audiobook)

Printed in the United States of America

—

Book Midwifery by Fen Druadin
Copyediting & Proofreading by James Gallagher
Illustrations by Monita Honar
Handwriting by Katrina Busselle
Author photo by Amy Kubik
Book Design & Publishing by Kory Kirby
SET IN MR EAVES MOD OT

For Mom and Terry,

Wisdom
Perspective
Laughter
Empathy
Living boldly

First, I learned from you.

Contents

Introduction

I wrote this book to prove to myself that I could.

WHO AM I?

My life experience, so far, is that of a fifty-four-year-old white woman of privilege. Mother of two, divorced, been through some shit, I have figured some shit out too. I'm a formally trained mediator, leader of teams, and business-growth whisperer.

The stories I share in this book are based on my core beliefs and experience:

- I believe inspiration and insight come from everywhere. Be open.
- I believe in knowing what matters and spending your time doing more of that.

- I believe there is no right way of doing or being. Do it your way.
- I believe all relationships (including my relationship with myself) are founded on listening.
- I believe in action and checklists.
- I believe in sleep.
- I believe in taking leaps. Being uncomfortable, terrified, and excited comes with the territory of leaping.
- I believe in living like you know you're going to die.

Here's an important disclaimer about the ideas in this book—and a nod to my shrill librarian, whom you will meet. Thank you, shrill librarian. :)

These pages are not every woman's story, or most women's stories, or some women's stories. Only mine. I'm writing for myself to prove I can.

SPOTLIGHT DODGER

Want to know a secret? I've never wanted to be in the spotlight.

I'm GREAT at getting other people ready for the spotlight.

Katrina, the Spotlight *Supporter*. If you were going out on stage, here's a checklist I'd hand you. I love me a checklist for someone else to follow.

❏ Practice sessions complete (check)
❏ Breakfast eaten (check)
❏ Water on stage (check)
❏ Perfect outfit (check)
❏ Deodorant applied? (check) Twice? (check)
❏ Throat lozenges sucked (check)
❏ Mantra repeated (check)

My preferred role is nodding and supporting from the wings, ready to assist if something goes amok.

But me, up there under those hot lights? Nope.

Ha! Until now. Until this book.

Through this creative work, and because of the people who support me in this journey, I now am front-and-center stage, telling stories.

See me? I'm perched on that high stool in the perfect outfit, water at my side. Thank you!

I'm looking into the lights, delivering the goods, and being vulnerable.

Imagine that.

My glorious community supports and encourages me from the wings.

I'm Katrina, the woman you see up there on stage under the lights, sweating a bit. (Deodorant applied. Twice. Check.)

I did it by finding my one reason. And maybe you can too.

HOW TO ENGAGE WITH THIS BOOK: JUMP IN AND SCRIBBLE!

If you do only one thing, whip out a pen and do the opening *Million Reasons* exercise that follows.

Taking stock, noticing, and reflecting are the foundational stories of **Part One**.

Flush with insights and goals, you'll find the rubber meets the road in **Part Two** as I explore taking action and navigating inevitable obstacles.

Part Three features the themes of reckoning with reality and letting go. **Part Four** is a battle cry to get up from setbacks and keep living.

But let's face it: change often feels like a chaotic vortex.

So "read" this book however you like. Permission granted.

One advance reader spent weeks inspired and meditatively reading sections separately and reflecting along the way.

Another woman devoured these pages in one session while taking an afternoon walk. She sent me a picture of her walking and reading 8½ x 11" pieces of white paper—can you believe that? Yes, those reading-and-walking people exist.

Are you having a shit day? Or have you carved out an hour to do something important and are proud of yourself? I'd be honored to be your companion and your cheerleader. The sections are short. Scribble in the margins, underline, or not.

I end most sections with a question or reflection. The blank pages welcome your ink; you've got space, but take more if you need it. If you are listening to this, grab a notebook. Have at it.

Permission granted, any way you want.

My only hope is that one idea or story will speak to you. One reason why you can. Anything else is gravy.

Here are three bonus beliefs:

- I believe in possibility.
- I believe in positivity.
- And, although we haven't yet met, I believe in you.

Million Reasons

GRAB A PEN: IT STARTS WITH ONE REASON

At its essence, this book is about taking stock and taking action.

And getting out of your own way.

This **"One Reason You Can"** reflection is a beginning place.

First, make a list of things you'd like to do. Or how you'd like to be in the world. You don't need to know how. Release your imagination.

Examples: leave my job, travel to Asia, communicate better with my spouse, get pissed at my kids less, start an MBA, double my revenue in three years, be a better listener, play pickleball twice a week.

You go . . .

Things I'd like to do/bc:

Now list a million reasons (well, it doesn't actually need to be a million) why you can't do those things.

Examples: I don't have the time, money, transportation. I don't have any experience doing "x." People like me don't do "x." I'm too short, fat, tall, old, awkward, sick. My job is demanding. With children and aging parents, finding time for myself is impossible. I work two jobs and barely get by. English isn't my native language; people won't understand me. I suffer from debilitating depression. I'm in constant physical pain. I have no idea who I am, what I want, or the changes I want to make. I suck at "x." I'll never be able to do that. I'm too scared. I have no fucking money and am in debt up to my ears. It would take too long.

What are your million reasons? The million reasons why you can't do the items from your first list plus anything else? Let it rip.

Why I can't do those things:

These, and others, are real reasons you can't. Concrete. Understandable. Legitimate.

I honor and respect your list. Notice some come from inside you and others from the broader culture and where you were born, when you were born, and to whom you happen to have been born.

Taken as a whole, these stories are stopping you. You see that, right?

With all the reasons you *can't* now written down on paper, go back to your first **like to do/be list** and pick one thing that matters to you; then give yourself one reason why you can. Just one.

One reason why I can:

That's all you need, one reason.

A seed.

A possibility.

It builds from there.

Welcome to the journey of the possible.

The Million Reasons Why I Wasn't Going to Write This Book

I had a million reasons not to write this book, starting with high school.

Anytime I wrote anything, it felt like I would be hit with a series of knuckle raps for not following the rules.

Fail to structure my opening paragraph properly?

Thwock.

Or, later in life, the business proposal is not detailed or technical-sounding enough?

"Ouch."

My relationship to writing is complicated, as my knuckles can attest.

Last January I emceed a workshop about writing the book "inside of you."

Inside of me?

Nope, not me.

Other people have books inside of them. I planned to be a fly on the wall.

Unexpectedly, I participated.

What happened in the workshop was as foreign as taking mushrooms in the desert or speaking in tongues. I found myself dancing down the proverbial aisle, my hands flung skyward. "I do have a book in me!"

The facilitators led a visualization exercise as part of the workshop, and I found myself saying my future book title aloud: "*A Million Reasons Why You Can't!*" I could see the spine of the book in front of me. I imagined a hand, your hand, reaching for it.

After the euphoria wore off, it was as if my book said, "The next move is yours, Katrina. Do you want to do this?"

Cue the chorus of a million reasons why I couldn't write a book.

"You have nothing to say."

"You're unqualified."

"Who the hell is going to be interested in your book?"

"Other people in the family are writers, not you . . ."

You get the idea.

The voices inside my head debated for a few days.

I mentioned my workshop experience to my friends and community, and they all said, "I can't wait to read that book."

Really? Cue a confused look and head scratch.

A brave, strong, sage part inside me piped up and said, "Yes, you can. People want to read it. You'll get help with the process. You won't be alone. Make it what you want. Your voice and format. Ha, if no one else, your mom and friends will read it."

"Your writing. Your rules."

"Try."

"It's time. You can do this."

You need only one reason.

So you're reading or hearing this book right now . . .

Because I wrote it. It's one of the hardest things I've ever done. But I did it, because I needed only that one reason.

I dedicate this work to you and to doing daunting and challenging things.

Yes, you can.

And you need only one reason to believe it.

A
Million
Reasons
Why
You
Can't

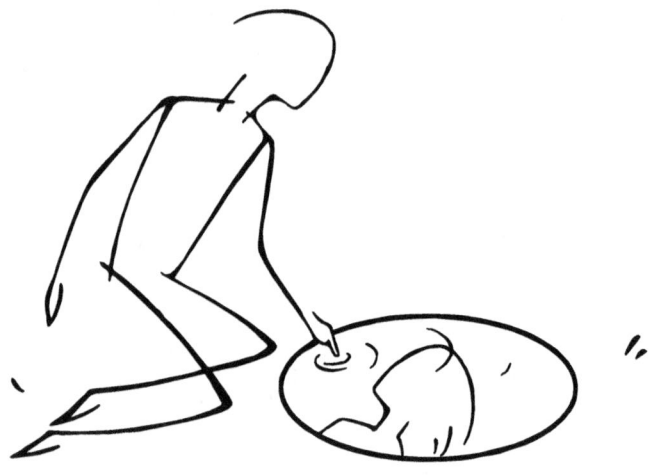

PART I

NOTICE, REFLECT & FOCUS

Under what circumstances do you have aha moments, ideas, and insights?

Sometimes insights come because you create space. For example, I write thirty minutes a day. I create the space, and the insights and work follow. Therapy is a structured environment. If I go on a retreat, I welcome new ideas.

Cal Newport, author of *Deep Work*, provides strategies for setting aside time and days to think and work deeply.[1] To create.

Other times, insights feel random and unstructured. You might have an idea in the shower. When those creative moments happen, be open to where they take you.

For example, a dear friend was walking with her wife and mentioned the empty office space next to hers. Creatively, tugging on that thread of the vacant office beside hers, she mused, "I could rent that

---

1 Cal Newport's book *Deep Work* is an inspiring and actionable work on the topic of how to make deep work happen.

space." Continuing, she gained momentum, saying out loud that maybe it was time to start the group practice. The idea had been simmering in her mind for ages.

Days later, like that, she leaped. Today she's building a group practice. The inspiration? A conversation, an empty office, and wanting to take the month of August off.

Perfect.

How about another important sign to tune in and reflect?

Being scared shitless.

Feel scared; be curious.

Brené Brown[2] says that fear and vulnerability always accompany bravery.

Your inspiration will come from different sources, and I dedicate this "Notice, Reflect & Focus" section to tuning in.

---

2 Brené Brown, *Rising Strong* (New York: Random House, 2015).

Recharging &
Replenishing

Mountain hikes recharge me.

    With stories or podcasts in my ears, I zigzag straight up the mountain for twenty minutes. I use hiking poles (for years I thought they were dorky; now I love them) and work around high rocks and mud. Panting and sweaty, I stop and rest at the overlook at the top. I admire the majestic and twisting Hudson River, notice the trees in their season and the houses nestled amid the mountains. For my descent, my headphones are tucked away. Poles planting rhythmically to keep me standing, I listen to the sounds of the forest, my feet crunching and sliding. My body's in motion, flowing downhill, exertion behind me. A clear mind. A glorious reset. I'm alive.

A rejuvenating mix for me? Exertion, nature, focus, and awe.

Introverts need time alone.

Surfers live for the water and waves.

Chefs experiment with new ingredients and recipes.

Have you figured out what you need to recharge and replenish?

You might be thinking, *What's this recharging shit? That's for other people; I've got a million reasons why I can't attend to myself. Let's start with the fact I'm fucking exhausted. With small children, a demanding job, home responsibilities, illness, caregiving, and financial stress, you fill in the blanks.*

I hear you, BUT ignoring what you need exacts a price.

It depletes you.

Consider a challenge. Identify one thing that recharges you. Then find a way to do it.

Take a walk in nature. Listen to a favorite song and sing your lungs out. Sit in the park and watch the pigeons. Go for a drive. Take that class.

Learn to make a chocolate soufflé. Get your mother-in-law to watch your children so you can get away for a weekend. Start a book club.

Paint with your fingers and toes. Look out your window and notice what's out there.

Recharging gives you perspective and freedom. It feeds your soul.

What's one small thing
you can do today or tomorrow
to care for yourself & recharge?

From "Fuck No!" to "Fuck Yes!"

The process of going from "Fuck no!" to "Fuck yes!" can take seconds, minutes, months, years—heck, a lifetime.

Behavioral scientists study what it takes for people to make behavioral changes, and it turns out there is a sequence:[3]

- Precontemplation (you don't intend to take action)
- Contemplation (intending to start)
- Preparation (ready to take action)
- **Action (changing the behavior)**
- Maintenance (sustaining)

3 J. O. Prochaska and C. C. DiClemente, "Stages and Processes of Self-Change of Smoking: Toward an Integrative Model of Change," *Journal of Consulting and Clinical Psychology* 51, no. 3 (1970): 390–395.

Look at that! Three out of five steps happen BEFORE action.

Often we focus on the bit of the iceberg sticking up called "action"—but there's plenty that we can't see.

A shout-out to the process of noticing, reflecting, and getting ready.

What changes are you starting
To Think about making?

PART II:

TAKE ACTION & NAVIGATE OBSTACLES

So you are ready! Or as ready as you can be. You've worked through "no way" to "intending to start" to "getting ready to start."

You're ready for action.

Let's explore what it takes to make action stick.

Because just wanting to isn't enough.

It's change. And it's hard as fuck.

Maybe it doesn't have to be as hard. Maybe.

The Secret? Do MORE of What Matters Most

Can we talk about today? It's bonkers and raining. My work is jammed with tasks and meetings. My son and I need to talk about college with the guidance counselor. My daughter suddenly wants to go on a road trip to see colleges next week, so I need to shuffle a bunch of shit. In other words, I have a million reasons why I can't attend my exercise class.

And yet I get up from my desk, mid-email, and go to my spin class. Do you know spin? Where people of all shapes and ages pack into close quarters, sweat, and ride bikes to nowhere as music pounds? (Trust me, I wear earplugs.) Yup, that's me today.

I do it because exercise matters. And I am committed.

If I don't prioritize myself, my health, my family and

friends, and the things that matter, I'll be capsized by the needs of others: relentless tasks and responsibilities.

You know there is always more work.

Domestic work, parenting, your job—you never actually finish. So if you never finish, what's the goal? What's the point?

Ready for it? The goal of life is to do more of what matters.

Prioritize it.

As Oliver Burkeman, author of *Four Thousand Weeks*, wisely says, "What you pay attention to will define, for you, what reality is."

If travel is important to you, start an account to pay for it, put money aside, identify dates, and book it.

If you want to write, start writing. Want support? Join a writing group or an online community, or hire a writing coach.

Want to be at your daughter's soccer games? Figure out how to adapt and prioritize so you'll be there.

Are you squeezed and stressed at work and want to change jobs? Get on it.

Carving out the time, energy, and money to fund what matters is hard.

It is hard as fuck.

But you can. It turns out you **are** the accumulation of your habits.

"Every action you take is a vote for the type of person you wish to become. No single instance will transform your beliefs, but as the votes build up, so does the evidence of your new identity."

— JAMES CLEAR, author of *Atomic Habits*

What can you do—or do
you do—every day to
engage with what matters?

Can I Get a Little Help over Here?

Taking action and maintaining your momentum is supported by getting help. Help can come in three ways:

1. Pay for it (virtual assistant, therapist, personal trainer, caregiver, coach, housecleaner).
2. Barter for it (babysitting cooperatives, "You walk my dog, I'll water your plants").
3. Get it for free (caregiving, emotional support, accountability).

PAY FOR IT

I work with solo consultants who have built their businesses doing everything themselves. At a certain point, though, this is no longer sustainable. Imagine taking their laptops to bed and having no days off. "I've got too much to do" is a common refrain. A lure of the consulting life is freedom, yet they are too busy to tend to their lives, especially their personal lives.

"Something's gotta give."

Help! They need to hire help, and I walk them through the process. Most often their first hire is a virtual assistant to take administrative tasks off their plates. Administrative tasks are the easiest to pry out of their hands. Pulling the trigger is always scary (*Can I afford it? Can I trust them?*).

Then they leap. The result? A better life and a stronger business.

Pay for help—an assistant, therapist, coach, housecleaner, personal trainer, or caregiver. A food-delivery service could help get dinner on the table a few days a week.

BARTER FOR IT

My mother is an accomplished author (also a photographer and videographer). Here's a bragging interlude of her accomplishments:

Photo-editing a seven-hundred-page cookbook.

Writing two young adult novels and one work of nonfiction.

Doing a stint as a staff writer and photo editor for a photography magazine.

Today, when she wants to, she writes articles (and does the photographs and videos) for *Martha's Vineyard Magazine*.

Bartering sparked the writing chapter of her life.

In her midforties, Mom saw a flyer for a women's writing workshop entitled "Women Writing, Women Telling." She didn't have time (three children and a household to run), money (we were strapped), or writing experience. Yet she'd always wanted to write and wondered whether she could figure out a way. Yes! She and the teacher bartered—the writing workshop for publicity photos.

That bartered workshop ignited her writing career.

A million reasons why she couldn't (too old, no experience, no money, no time). A swap, a passion for the craft, hard work, and she was on her way.

GET IT FOR FREE: THE KINDNESS OF OTHERS

My friend Phyl (they/them) was a life raft when my kids were in kindergarten. I mentioned wanting to attend a Zumba class on Thursdays. "How about I pick up the kids on Thursdays and amuse them so you can go to your class?" Sold! Bless. They did this for years. They did it to help me, yes. And also because they didn't have children and wanted to spend time with two little people who were, and are still, quite spectacular.

People like to help—it feels good. They do it for their own reasons.

Ask for help. Accept the offers. Phyl's lifework is dedicated to encouraging millions to ask for and receive help. They've written a fabulous book on asking for help and the job-search process: *Never Search Alone* by Phyl Terry. It's a game changer.

Here's a challenge: as you focus on what matters most, consider what can come off your plate and how other people can help.

Stuck? Get help with that!

What do you need help with?

Goals & Habits

Order it now if you haven't read *Atomic Habits* by James Clear. A central message is that it's not about achieving a specific goal (for example, making 300K or losing fifty pounds); it's about your systems and focus. Action toward what matters. Repeatable, small, sustainable, satisfying habits.

Here's a recent example of focusing on a flawed and failed goal of "learning Italian."

I'm in love with an Italian. He's lived in New Jersey for more years now than he lived in Italy. Massimo is one of ten children from a small village outside of Naples. His siblings are teachers, merchants, photographers, health aides, and even a yoga and volleyball coach.

For all their talents, they speak almost no English.

I speak no Italian.

I met his family last August and watched them talk—a highly entertaining activity complete with hand gestures I'd seen only in the movies. As much as I amused myself with their self-expression and concentrated on catching a few words here or there, I was lost and often discouraged. Not understanding is tiring, frustrating, and lonely.

Returning home, I proclaimed an ambitious goal to myself and my loved ones: "I'm going to learn Italian!"

Diving in, I hired an online tutor from Naples. She focused on grammar and rote memorization (I hate both), and when I screwed up, which I did ALL THE TIME, she shook her finger at me ("No, no, no") and clicked her tongue.

Discouraged, I knew I was failing fast. After a particularly agonizing session, I burst into tears. "Christ, Katrina, this is supposed to be fun." I noted the chorus of negativity and why I couldn't continue "learning Italian."

"You are truly terrible at this."

"Spanish is hardwired in your brain; you'll never get Italian."

"Your brain is old."

"Why bother? You can study forever, and you'll never be able to converse."

"Lost cause."

I didn't quit.

I recalculated.

I adopted a new goal, better systems, and a growth mindset.

New goal: engage with the Italian language. Notice: *engage*, not "learn." I told myself, "Next time you go to Italy, Katrina, you'll have more language."

System: Italian once a week for an hour. With a teacher who's perfect for me.

Mindset: a mental workout. Have fun. Whatever makes it into your brain, bravo!

Cheerful, engaging, and doable.

I got a new tutor, Emanuele. We meet on Thursday mornings at 8:00 a.m. (help and a doable system). When a word in Spanish comes to my brain, Emanuele nods understandingly, gives me the word in Italian, and encourages me. We joke, laugh, and talk about pizza.

My revised goal is "engagement" with Italian, not "learning." My systems and mindset ensure I'm challenged, engaged, and having a good time. After every lesson, I'm energized. Growth mindset—let's go!

The doubter voices don't have a chance. I changed the game.

Think about small, doable steps and moving onward.

Read *Atomic Habits* and go deeper.

Go ahead & break down
something big & daunting
into manageable & satisfying
bites. Try

The Power of Other People's Positivity

Mornings are usually my favorite time—I'm fresh, cheerful, and optimistic about my day.

Today that shit's not flowing. I slept late, Benadryl-drugged from getting back to sleep at midnight. My brain is foggy. Hair standing straight up, I head to the coffeepot.

Unknown to me, my business partner, Max Traylor, started his day writing a LinkedIn post dedicated to me and what I bring to our partnership.

So I drop off the kids and stumble to my computer with more caffeine. I open my inbox and LinkedIn to a flood of people shouting out my fabulousness.

"Katrina Busselle has made a huge difference in my life too! She's truly one of a kind. Brilliant, focused, supportive and a world-class accountability partner. I'm also blessed to be able to call her a friend. I could keep going but I have to finish that checklist she wants from me."

— SUSAN T

"Katrina Busselle is a force!! She has helped me in so many ways, not just with her expertise but her compassion and damn good nature. Big love to her."

— CAROLINE C

"Katrina Busselle is an absolute rock star (sorry, Gene Simmons, but it's true). If I could work with her every day I would. She has an incredible operational brain, keeps us focused and on schedule, and is just an amazing woman."

— JESSICA G

I'm going to have a kick-ass day. The evidence is there!

It's great when it works out like this, but you can't count on someone to post a message and the community to build you up when needed.

So, what to do? Keep those love letters. Print 'em. Have a drawer for that gold. Pin them on your wall.

Copy and paste into a file. People give you appreciation and kudos for who you are and what you contribute. It can be a perfect boost for when you feel low. Or anytime! Sometimes you're feeling great and want to be reminded.

Harness the positive words of others.

Ask your colleagues & friends to share positive things about you. What do they say?

How do you tap into the energy of those wonderful things they say?

Another Shitty Morning?

A REFLECTION ON POWERING THROUGH

I write first thing in the morning, so you'll get a second example of starting the day on the wrong foot and the turnaround.

I'm actively feeling shitty and smiling as I write this. I'm smiling because I know I'm on my way out. But I'm still feeling shitty. Promise not to judge? Do you want to hear my reasons?

My pork vindaloo is too salty.

It took me three hours, and goddamn it—it's just too salty. And I know I need to go out and buy the ingredients again and start over so I'll have it for an Indian-themed dinner I'm hosting.

Then I'm making croutons, and they burn. I can't find a fucking airtight lid for a plastic container: Why do the lids never fit? Really? *Really?* And I'm on a waiting list for a morning spin class (fucking waiting list). And I'm checking it, and I didn't get in.

My hair is sticking out in all directions. I'm growing it out to a bob—God help me. Looking in the mirror, I see that my face is washed out, and I keep forgetting to dye my eyebrows. I called Massimo to see if he could come over for a hike this afternoon, but he has too much to do. My kitchen smells like vindaloo (and not in a good way). Do you get it? I know you do. I can feel you nodding along.

What's a girl to fucking do? And what kind of problems are these? On a different day I'd laugh them all off. "Oh well."

Before setting my timer to write, I descend to the downstairs bathroom. Wetting my face and hair, I begin taming my locks with super-hold gel (love that stuff). Usually not a makeup person, I pull out my little baggie of cosmetics and go to work. I have mascara-type stuff for my eyebrows. Now they are dark brown and shapely instead of washed out. My liquid eyeliner is cooperating, and I have fine black lines in the right spots. Next, a coat of mascara for my pale and average eyelashes. I apply my shimmery pink Burt's Bees to my cheeks, rub in the tint, and smell the light peppermint. Finally, I pucker up and put the heavenly pink peppermint on my lips. I'll keep on my black turtleneck and stay in my comfortable COVID sweats.

Finally, I select a pair of eyeglasses. Thanks to inexpensive purveyors in China, I've got about six pairs to choose from. The bold red-rimmed ones appeal. I pick an equally splashy pair of fire-engine-red plastic chandelier earrings—and I'm done. Here we are, and I'm all gussied up, just for me. Today, this is the perfect first step in the right direction.

We all wake up in shitty moods sometimes, or the day turns shitty. Or something stressful and hard is happening in your life. Sometimes I go with it—fuck it, I'm out. I'm going to bed, lying low. Calling in sick. A TV splurge, Cheetos—that's a legit choice.

Other times we can trick our brains, hormones, and bodies into a turnaround.

Know what those levers are for you. For me, I try sprucing up my look, exercising, and reaching out to a friend or a partner and saying out loud, "I'm in a bad fucking mood," and talking about it. It helps; it just does.

Journal, meditate, and do something nice for someone else. Do something delightful for yourself. Get out into the sunshine.

Of course, there's a place for feeling low. Spend time there if that's what the situation calls for.

Today I'm moving out of it and getting on with my precious life.

So see, I just did it—and I know you can too.

When you want to get
out of a funk, what
actions (internal or external)
do you take?

What "Action" or "Ready" Can Look Like

Massimo is a terrific father, the number-one salesperson at his company. In my book, he wins the sexiest, kindest, and most-awesome-boyfriend-ever award.

He's also overweight and struggles to care for himself physically.

From the beginning of our relationship, I've been "encouraging" him (okay, let's call it what it is, mostly nagging) to get active. For Christmas during our second year together, I got him a gym membership—which he canceled two months later because he wasn't going. I urge him regularly to get up from his desk and speed walk around his suburban New Jersey neighborhood. *Move!*

Although not deaf ears, he can't make the change—as

you may have seen, the stages of behavioral change have five parts:

1. Precontemplation
2. Contemplation
3. Preparation
4. Action
5. Maintenance

Note: you don't get to "action" until the fourth!

I've been working hard on myself and my reactions. I can't change Massimo. He will make health changes when he's ready.

Last May, when he went in for a pre-op blood workup before getting his deviated septum fixed, his GP told him he was prediabetic and his cholesterol levels sucked. Although clearing him for his operation, the doctor handed him two scripts, a diabetes-prevention drug and another drug to address his cholesterol. "You need to take these medications from now on."

On the phone to me hours later, Massimo was adamant: "I'm not going to take drugs. I can do this on my own. I need to change the way I eat and exercise."

That was the moment.

He began doggedly researching and listening to

podcasts, learning about diabetes and controlling sugar, eating differently, and even fasting. He's committed to losing weight, changing his eating, and moving. He's starting with two- to three-mile walks.

"No drugs" spurred him to action. He's determined to avoid medication.

He's doing it.

Thinking back over your life...
What tips you from "thinking
about it" or "Wanting to do it"
TO → "DOING IT?"

Can you engineer more of
those moments for yourself
for the things that matter?

Oh Fuck, My Brain/Body Doesn't Work That Way

In my youth, I loved science, test tubes, and plumes of smoke. How about those stars and planets? Seismic activity is happening right under our feet!

I was a *Science Girl*, engaged and confident. I applied myself and loved it.

Then came tenth grade and chemistry. Dazed and irrevocably lost after the first week, I clung on, confidence waning daily. No amount of extra help worked, and I ultimately dropped the course.

I know you can relate.

You discover—perhaps suddenly, perhaps not—that your brain can't do "x," or you hate "x." Now what?

If you must do that thing, figure out ways to get help and get through it.

Pay a tutor. Watch YouTube, and maybe draw a picture. Acknowledge that it is hard for your brain and explore alternative routes to get you through. For example, I took statistics as a one-on-one course. My professor's patience, humor, and tenacity got me through.

Or don't do it.

Consider what your brain and body can't do (or hate doing) and figure out another way.

Do you need to exercise but hate going to the gym? The options are endless: stairs, skipping rope, or speed walking outdoors.

If spelling and grammar elude you (as they do me), get your precious thoughts on paper, then utilize technology and the proofing skills of others. I'm never going to be a good speller—so move on. I have spell-check, Grammarly, and my friend Martha when it counts.

We all have shortcomings. Move through, move around, reframe, and get others to help.

Deficiencies are like quicksand. If you stagnate in your inadequacies, you're goin' down. So instead say to yourself, "All right, I see there's quicksand. What can I do?"

Your worst option is wading right in, thinking it will be different this time, and feeling yourself sink into the muck.

What are the other options?

Throw a plank over and walk quickly?

Go around and avoid it?

Back up and take a flying leap?

You got this! Troubleshoot that shit.

Think about a shortcoming
you are struggling with now.
What are your options?
Can you go around, over,
through or past it?

What Do You Need to Get Shit Done?

Everybody needs structure.

The key? Know yourself and what you need. Put yourself in optimal conditions.

Telling my son to "clean up his room" will yield nothing. Telling my son his room needs to be clean by 5:00 p.m. on Sunday and providing him a checklist of what "clean" means will yield an 80 percent success rate. Add a threat I'm prepared to carry out? One hundred percent. As a parent, that's the winning formula for him.

Like my son, the deadline-driven person needs a fixed and reinforced target—the quintessential newspaper deadline. The paper goes to print in thirty minutes; if you want your cover story, finish that shit.

What about the perfectionists? They work on it. Rewrite

it. Don't like it. Anguish. Rework the second paragraph one more time. Never enough time or effort. That's also problematic.

The perfectionist needs to limit the time they put into an activity (for example, you don't have twelve hours; you have two). At two hours, like a reality TV cooking show, you raise your hands and send it to the judges.

My jam is structuring my day by allocating time for certain activities. I'm writing this book in thirty-minute increments most days. Committing to thirty minutes allows me to say, "I did it. And tomorrow I'm on to the next part." At peace with the loose threads—they will be there tomorrow.

Atomic Habits says the person who plugs away with relatively easy, doable actions (for example, writing thirty minutes a day) has more chance of success (writing their book) than someone who bites off a bigger (often unsustainable) chunk.

> Know yourself and put yourself in the climate you need to engage productivity and get shit done.

What do you know
about yourself &
The structure you Need
To get stuff done?

On the Topic of Zs

Let's talk about sleep.

I've always been an early bird. Protected my sleep.

In college, by 8:00 p.m., if not sooner, my brain would be toast—worse, I'd be tilting toward worry. "What about that paper I haven't started?" I'd hear that worry playlist start up in my mind. What's the solution? Rest.

I'd lower the blinds, turn on my sound machine, and get cozy in my hard futon with a down mattress topper. Like a cozy puppy, I'd nestle in and sleep—a blissful reset. My alarm sounded at 4:30 a.m. I'd stumble to the coffeepot. Fueled by coffee, in my pj's, I'd start writing that paper. Pumped as they come. Blinds thrown open, I'd watch the sun come up. Splashing inspiration on the page, I'd have a good three to four hours under my belt while everyone else pried their eyes open at 9:00 or 10:00 a.m. after working late into the night.

So the wisdom isn't about being a morning person or a night owl—it's about the seven to eight hours between.

In my observation, night owls are often sleep deprived. The world tends to start before they are rested. However, night owl adults can make their natural rhythms work. How about midmorning start times and second or third shifts?

I know some people don't have the luxury of sleep. New parents, doctors in rotation, shift workers, police, sick folks, people working two or three jobs to make ends meet. If you are sleep deprived and there's little you can do about it, take care of your body as best as you can and set up firm boundaries (and sleeping conditions) so when you can sleep, you do.

A shout-out to the perimenopausal and menopausal women (like me). Menopause has fucked with our sleep. Try as we might, we can't sleep as we did before; it's hormonal. It's normal. It sucks. For men, aging prostates also lead to more interrupted sleep due to nocturnal visits to the can.

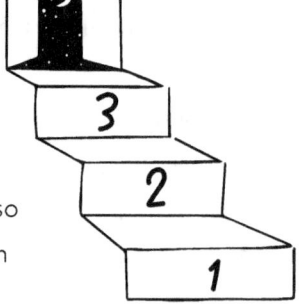

Sleep is personal. And it's so fucking important. Take action to improve your sleep—educate yourself, go see your doctor, and talk to your friends about what they do. This one really matters.

Why aren't you getting enough sleep? zzzzz

I Meet My Shrill Librarian

This is my first book pregnancy, and like all new parents, I have no idea what I'm doing.

My book midwife, Fen Druadìn, is experienced and fabulous. They've (Fen's pronouns are they/them) guided hundreds of books into the world.

After reading my first draft, Fen was brimming with encouragement. They also warned that the second draft is the most challenging for most authors.

Yup. My second draft was painful. Fen sent a word cartoon of the creative process so I could laugh and know my feelings and difficulties were expected. Originally created by Marcus Romer, it goes like this:

THE CREATIVE PROCESS

1. This is awesome.

2. This is tricky.
3. This is shit.
4. I am shit.

5. This might be okay.

6. This is awesome.

Perfectly said. I was wading through "This is tricky; this is shit; I am shit."

To help me navigate the blocks that were coming up for me, Fen offered a visualization workshop.

The visualization exercise was about identifying the part of me (the saboteur) piping up noisily and impeding my writing.

After relaxing and centering, Fen asked me whether I could identify the part of my body where I felt the dissonance.

I answered quickly, "My head." They asked me if I was sensing or hearing something in my head.

Tuning in, I replied, "Yes."

"What?"

"I'm hearing a shrill 'shh' sound and seeing a finger wagging."

Fen repeated, "You're hearing a 'shh' sound and seeing a finger wagging; tell me more."

"She's a librarian!"

Fen asked whether we could ask my shushing, finger-waving librarian self what she was saying.

"Be careful. Be careful. There are millions of people with other life experiences. They won't relate to you. They will judge you. Be careful. You need to follow the rules."

— SHRILL LIBRARIAN

Fen explained my "shh" self is a part of me. This part is trying to protect me from hurt and criticism. That's okay. I can't (we can't) make her go away.

As a moving-forward strategy, Fen suggested that if I was open to it, I could speak with my librarian before I started writing. Keep her informed and hear her thoughts. Then write.

I've been inviting her in, smiling in welcome. I referenced her in an earlier section and even gave her props.

Incredible.

Have you ever tried talking to the parts of you that are problematic or impeding your progress or process? It's like a séance of one—conjuring people/voices and asking them questions.

This may sound out there, but give it a try.

Coaches, therapists, and wise humans also facilitate.[4]

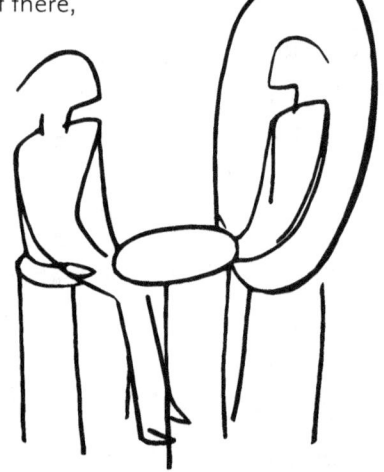

---

4 This is an emerging therapeutic framework called Internal Family Systems.

Can you describe a voice inside
you that delivers sometimes shrill
(or negative or cautionary) messages
in service of protecting you? What
happens if you invite it to join you?

When You Start Failing, Renegotiate

I've been working away on this book a set amount of time every weekday, no matter what. If the words make sense, great. If they are fucking shit, that's cool as well. The writing itself is the win.

On Friday, though, I have to get a sonogram of my boob (it's fine). I need to lead a workshop, then tie up a few last-minute threads and flat out sprint to catch the train to meet Massimo for a romantic getaway in NYC.

I didn't write. I skipped a day—I had a million good reasons, didn't I?

Yes, it's okay. But I'm afraid I'll slip and throw in the towel if I'm not doing it daily.

Last night I watched a survival show. Pontoon planes drop contestants into the rainforest of Alaska with only the clothes on their backs and a few supplies. First they have to scramble for shelter and fire. Then the gnawing hunger sets in. They can't seem to catch an errant salmon with a jerry-rigged soda-can-top hook. They eat found mussels and limpets (*Ever heard of a limpet? It's like a barnacle, I think*) harvested from the beach. When they can no longer take it, they fire a flare gun into the air—symbolizing to all the competitors that another person has succumbed and left the competition.

A hard-bitten private investigator in the real world turns to the camera and talks about the domino effect when the first person gives up and fires the flare into the air. She points out that the first person to eject from the competition gives power and momentum to the idea that it *is* possible to give up. That being starved, bone weary, smelly, and irritable (*Did I mention starved?*) could end with a brief incendiary.

Permission granted, contestants start falling like flies. "I just can't do it anymore" is the most common refrain.

Failure / "fuck it" isn't reserved for most New Year's resolutions. It's a fact of life.

As a fifty-plus-year-old, I've set out to do the following:

- Touch type: *Fail.*
- Remember people's names: *Fail.*
- Journal daily: *Fail.*

- Meditate on a regular basis: *Fail.*
- Do stuff on LinkedIn: *Fail.*
- Keep the basement and toolshed organized: *Fail.*

You get the idea. You have your list.

What's a girl to do?

Willpower is strongest out of the gate. However, will-power isn't enough and it won't power you through when you internally say, "Fuck this. This is too hard, and I give up." And although it is a relief, it also puts a notch into the belt of self-hatred and shame. One of those internal voices said, "I told you so." And those failures all add up.

What's the fucking answer? Pick a modest change, turn it into a habit, and try. Support yourself as best as you can.

I don't have this shit figured out. I just know it's Monday. It's okay I skipped Friday, but I'm back at writing—no flare and evacuation for me.

I'm modifying "writing for thirty minutes every day" to "writing for thirty minutes most days." That I can do.

And I am.

And now look: a book.

How can you modify something you're failing at today to make it simpler/smaller or achievable?

Reconcile & Rumble
with Your Impostor

Picture me at age twenty-one, in a rustic hotel in the Monteverde Cloud Forest of Costa Rica, a much-needed vacation celebrating my graduation from Hampshire College the week before. I'm weary of facing probing questions from everyone about my postcollege plans. Short answer: I don't have any.

A chunky black phone sounds in our hotel room in the early evening. After answering with a tentative "Hello," I learn that it's Terry, the executive director of the mediation center where I interned.

"I'm calling to offer you a full-time position as the community dispute resolution program director." I don't remember what she said after that. I yelped in assent—my dream job. We danced to celebrate; I relished my luck and twirled in joy.

The next day, still in the rainforest with parrots calling and iguanas sunning themselves on rocks, I woke up in the grip of doubt and guilt.

Hello, impostor.

I would be replacing Joan, who was in her forties, a bit of a pill, and a paralegal. In contrast, I was a (very) recent college graduate. Joan knew the ins and outs of the judicial system. I was just learning.

I was telling myself a million reasons why I was unqualified, was the wrong choice, and would suck at it.

It was a memorable case of impostor syndrome, and what a doozy. I took the job. I led the program for years. CEO Terry could see I was light-years better than Joan. I breathed life, structure, and innovation into a program that had gone stale.

Today, here's how I rumble with my impostor reaction, because it will happen.

First, I celebrate. For example, I will turn in this next draft and enjoy a few days of relief and exhilaration—yeah! I did it!

I know what's coming next, though. Self-doubt. Remember "This is shit; I'm shit"?

Knowing it's coming, I have strategies.

I face internal opposition like Wonder Woman facing

arrows. The doubts will come flying fast and true. Doubts from inside me directed at me. Some pierce the skin and embed. I deflect many, though, through balance, strength, and my shield of self-awareness.

The impostor is here to stay. You go, Wonder Woman!

How do you handle self doubt?

your favorite drink
might help! →

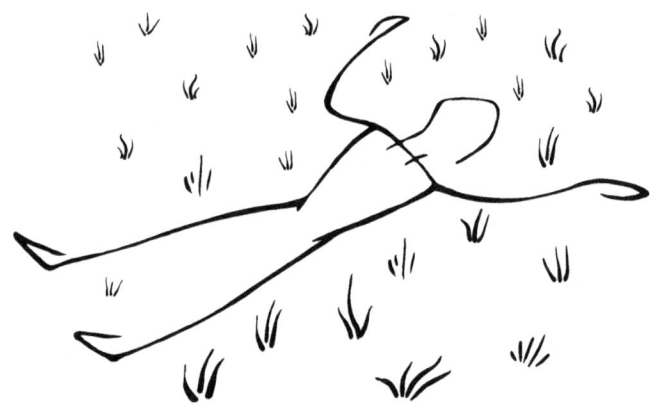

PART III:

RECKON
& LET GO

The Serenity Prayer popularized by Alcoholics
Anonymous is profound. I'll skip the opening "God"
word.

> "... grant me serenity to accept the things I cannot change;
> courage to change the things I can; and wisdom to know
> the difference."
>
> — REINHOLD NIEBUHR (1892–1971)

Let's break it down.

Accept the things you cannot change. *Okay.* ☑

Take action to change the things you can. *Got it.* ☑

Hold up. What the hell do you do with all the things
you thought you could change, but you can't? **?**

This section is dedicated to reckoning, the seemingly
miraculous act of letting go.

You Can't Change Other People. Consider Quitting.

I signed up for a lifetime with a man I thought I could change.

Yes, he's crusty and a bit of a pill, but he is a good person with a good heart. I signed up for battling, influencing, coaxing, and encouraging, trying to get him to change.

My marriage was exhausting.

Eventually I stopped expecting and asking. I let go.

When I let go of trying to change him, I created a space for myself within my marriage to feel peaceful and happy.

I'll give you an example: driving.

I'm a great driver.

Irrelevant.

Anytime I drove, the trip would be marked by unwanted and unsolicited feedback. He was anxious in the passenger seat: "Watch out for that car. The light is green." All sorts of "helpful" (not helpful) information and direction. You get the idea. I was pissed. Who does he think he is? I've been driving my whole life. Thinking the whole time, "Shut the fuck up!"

One day I told him, "I'm done. I'm done driving. I can't take the continuous suggestions and critique. You drive."

I became a passenger for the rest of our marriage. I had a chauffeur. If he got tired on a long trip, we got gas and a snack, and he climbed back behind the wheel.

I tried everything to counter his running critique. Then I left the battle, and it felt great.

Leaving the battle creates freedom. Letting go.

Here's the lesson: People are who they are. You can't change them.

Who can you change? Yourself. Look at your boundaries and strategies. Mind your own business. I recommend Byron Katie's book *The Work*. She gives you a framework to address your challenges instead of focusing on the deficiencies of others.

What can you change? More things than you can imagine. You are a boundless well of potential and actualization. Who can't you change? Others.

Stop trying and keep your eyes on your path. Only yours.

Focus on you. What can you change about your mindset?

What Letting Go Can Look Like

When my son was thirteen, he had a skateboarding accident and broke his left leg in two places and his collarbone. He spent three days in the hospital and his summer in a bed in the living room, leg elevated, endless television, hopping to the bathroom to take care of the essentials.

He was never an avid exerciser. At the time he only walked to the garage to play computer games. COVID settled in, as did depression, and he was a sullen, angry mess.

When his cast was finally off, his orthopedist told him that for recovery to start, he needed to begin moving again by walking around the block for five minutes and then increasing it over time.

I couldn't get him to move. I cajoled. Tried rewards.

Threats. I asked him every day whether he had moved. He just grunted and left the room.

After months of ineffectual prodding, I gave up. "I've had it. I'm done. Do whatever you want. If you want to sit around all day, this is your body and life. Your choice." He said he wanted an elliptical. We got him one. He didn't use it.

The battle between us was over. It was now his battle alone. His body, his health. I threw in the towel.

I let go. Really let go. I accepted that I could not change his relationship to exercise.

His physical health is 100 percent his.

Fast-forward about six months, and he gets a job busing tables and begins walking ten to twenty miles every weekend—he's moving and feeling better. A further flash to last fall when he announced out of the blue that he wanted to join the gym. He starts working out; he goes off his antidepressants.

As I write this, he's buff, strong, and energetic, and he works out almost daily.

My gift to myself was letting go. Letting go means honestly ditching the outcome.

It so happens he's discovered his body and exercise, but that discovery is his. He has a lifetime ahead to work through his physical health.

As it happened, he turned himself around. He very

well could have stayed stagnant and out of shape. His life, his decision.

Letting go is detaching. "Accepting the things you cannot change."

Here's a second example from my colleague and friend "Sarah."

Sarah and her little brother were never particularly close growing up.

In college her brother experienced the death of a close friend, and perhaps because of that, he began to direct a firehose of fury and hurt at her. He was angry but wouldn't talk about it directly. He wouldn't be in the same room with Sarah. When asked by their parents what was behind this, Sarah told me that the gist of it was, "I'm a bitch. He believes everything came easily to me in our childhood and that my parents treated me better than him. Basically, I was the source of all his problems."

Sarah was upset and committed to working it through with him. "What the heck, I'm a therapist! I wrote him a letter, sent him books, and even showed up at his house to get him to talk to me. My parents staged an intervention."

It didn't get better, though. "Nothing worked. Same anger and behavior."

After years of pain, Sarah realized, "I was the one suffering." So she gave up. She let go.

And now? Today: "Fuck it, I don't care anymore. No

guilt, no shame. There are awkward moments, but I'm great."

The situation doesn't need to change or get better. She could not force or influence a reconciliation.

Letting go is the antidote to pain and suffering.

It's how you get to serenity.

Let's go back to the quote.

". . . grant me serenity to accept the things I cannot change; courage to change the things I can; and wisdom to know the difference."

What's the problem with fighting battles you don't need to fight or cant win?

Our Minds & Bodies Are Aging, & It Sucks

One of my dearest friends turned sixty recently. At an intimate birthday celebration, during a reflective post-dinner coffee, her eyes filled with tears as she talked about her aging body. She illustrated this by squeezing her belly with two hands, showing us what she called her "paunch." This friend has a master's in public health, eats healthy food, and lives an active lifestyle. Even though she's doing everything right, her body is changing. The clothes in her closet don't fit like they did.

Our intimate group offered support and wisdom. We know. It's happening to all of us.

You are getting older, too, and your body is changing.

As I age, as you age, more will go south with our bodies: illness, aches, wrinkles, dimples, disease. Our bones shrink, our spines curve, and knuckles become gnarled with arthritis. Our minds don't work like they used to.

This shit is hard. If you continue to live into old age, it is not a question of "if" this will happen, but rather which elements will be the ones to bring on your natural death.

Aging is grief.

It seems to me the challenge is to feel the grief, acknowledge it, then move into acceptance and living.

Our lives are going in only one direction. Toward death. Accept the things you cannot change.

Why deny this reality?
Why not look at it straight on?[5]

Aging and death go
one way. We can fight
it or reconcile.

I'm working on making peace with the grief of aging. How about you?

Are You Waiting for Other People to Give You Permission?

When my twins were infants, I was in a sleep-deprived haze characterized by crying babies, endless feedings, pain, changing diapers, walks, visitors, and adjusting to the new realities of my life.

At three months, my twins were sleep trained. You know how important sleep is to me. I could now sleep for seven to eight hours. Ah, I felt like myself again.

After taking stock, even though my maternity leave was planned for six months, do you know what I wanted to do? Go back to work.

I craved my work colleagues and intellectual stimulation. Meetings. An office where no one was crying! The flexibility to pop out and get a salad or a Korean spicy seafood tofu soup.

I didn't have to be thrilled with the work and life of caring for our infant twins 24-7.

I called in the help of our beloved nanny, Graciella, and went back to work.

"Permission granted"[6] to go back. ***!!!***

The talented coach Beth Conger challenges us to determine what it would take to give permission to ourselves instead of seeking permission and validation from others. From our culture, from the outside.

You give yourself permission, a reason why you can do the following:

- Not go back to work.
- Go back to work.
- Write a book.
- Work for yourself.
- Start a group practice.
- Get a law degree at age fifty.

How do you grant yourself permission?

Like Byron Katie, Gianna Biscontini, MA, EdHD, BCBA, author of *Fuckless, a Guide to Wild Unencumbered Freedom*,

---

6 A phrase I attribute to the talented coach Beth Conger.

has prompts to get you to a permission-granted state she calls "living fuckless."

Biscontini's model for living fuckless includes first doing work on why you believe what you believe (aka your past, our culture, our history). Then letting go guided by these questions. Try using these questions like Mad Libs, but feel free to write sentences and paragraphs, not just a single word.

1. I'm dropping the belief that [*state belief here*].
2. Because [*reason*].
3. If I'm successful, what will happen [*be specific*].
4. If I'm successful, I'll have time and energy for [*be specific*].
5. And it will feel [*emotional state*].
6. My new belief is [*reframe old belief—or write brand spanking new belief here*].
7. I will show this by [*specific actions, words, phrases...*].

This work and these steps are nothing less than a guided path to freedom. Wholly executed by you.

The whole point is this: waiting around for the permission of your job, society, or family places the power elsewhere.

The power belongs to you. Take it.

Reflect on one thing you are
waiting for permission on.

What Not Giving a Fuck Looks Like

My present to myself for my fiftieth birthday was a women's yoga retreat in Costa Rica. My first retreat after practicing for twenty-five-plus years.

Out of fifteen women, I was the oldest by far. In honor of the occasion, I paid to stay in a boutique hotel nearby, and I didn't bunk up collectively with the rest of the gals. I needed the space and the privacy, and I had just turned fifty. Permission granted.

We all practiced yoga, and the vibe was energetic and positive. The women came from all over the US. I noticed most had tattoos and loved talking about them. Also, they loved their bodies. Hefty girls rocked crop tops and bikinis. Breasts of all types were untethered from bras.

Some armpits and legs rocked hair. I marveled at their freedom and palpable body self-love.

On our last night, we walked to a restaurant to celebrate. Our leader advised us to wear our bathing suits under our clothes because, at spots, we might need to wade into the water as the tide came in. The gals were all dolled up for our last evening: bright dresses, hair up, sparkle makeup.

As we walked to dinner, the sun glared down on us in our finery. Dripping sweat, we headed down the beach. One by one, the women started peeling off their clothes to their bathing suits and walking in the water to cool off. I wore a black wraparound dress and was sweating buckets. With ample thighs, midriff bulges, and cellulite, the gals disrobed to their bikinis. They didn't give a fuck. They were hot and free.

Inspired, I tugged at my center belt. Sliding it off easily, I removed my wrap dress and joined them in my bikini. Comfortable in our own skin and bodies—and cooler! Those young women didn't care what anyone else thought. Their bodies, their freedom. In the moment I, too, was free.

Can you think of a time when you didn't give a fuck & it felt fabulous & free?

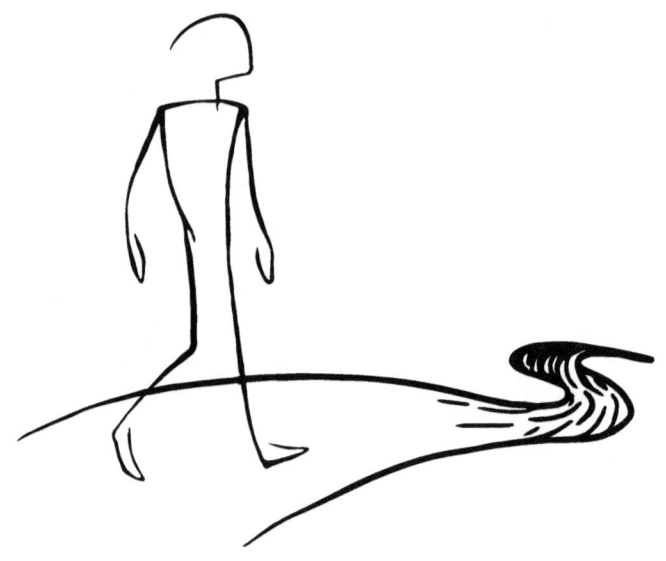

PART IV:

LIVE!

This final segment is dedicated to carrying on the best you can.

Shitty (and fabulous) things have happened and will continue to happen.

You may think you are in control (you're not).

Many believe we are guaranteed long and healthy lives if we do the "right" things.

I bet you know that's crap.

You can be a lifelong smoker and die in a car crash. A super-healthy person gets cancer. A stroke or a blood clot? *Poof.* A plane into a skyscraper. A casualty of a worldwide pandemic.

The truth is, you don't know when or how you're going to die. There's no guarantee for a "long and healthy" life.

So what can you control?

How you live.

When?

Today.

Getting Up after a "Face Down in the Arena"[7] Setback

The car nudges the grass as we pull up to the high school. My sixteen-year-old daughter, Alexandra, is biting her already raw lips. Tears glisten in her eyes. Hands tremble, and legs frantically bounce up and down.

A week ago her panic attacks went from occasional to debilitating. In the first days with acute panic, she followed me around the house like an anxious dog, from room to room. She slept in my bed. I witnessed her waking in a panic, bolt upright, crying and afraid.

---

7 A concept from *Rising Strong* and *Daring Greatly* from Brené Brown.

In the car, knowing it is time to go in, she looks at me with tear-worn eyes that plead, *Mom, I don't want to do this.*

A shaky glance at her phone shows it's time. She opens the car, grips her backpack, slings it over her shoulders, and walks toward the doors of her high school.

She's got a strategy and support for returning to school. With teachers in the know, she can leave class anytime. The social worker's office offers sanctuary. In her insulated lunch box lies an ice-cold face roller that helps shock her system. Her take-as-needed Xanax is also in her backpack, in a pillbox decorated with Frida Kahlo's self-portrait.

She has a million fucking reasons not to leave the car.

And she's doing it anyway.

She's fucking doing it.

No step is too small.

A million reasons why you can't. One reason and a strategy, and you are on your way.

You muster your shaky legs to carry you up the stairs, and ice-cold fingers grab the door handle. Perhaps you square your shoulders, blink back tears, and take a deep breath. And you've done it—just like my brave girl this morning.

Yes, you can!

Epilogue: On the Gift of Waking Up Alive

I knew Janet when she was a family mediator thirty years ago. She was a miracle worker with recalcitrant teenagers, even though she was "old." At age ninety, Janet continues her volunteer service as a Planned Parenthood clinic escort. A widow with family close by, she lives independently.

I interviewed her for an article I wrote during COVID and asked how she spends her time. "Katrina, I wake up surprised and delighted to be alive every morning. It seems I'm getting another day. What a blessing."

You, too, woke up this morning alive.

I hope you are awake to your dreams and how you want to live, awake to the possibilities of today.

You have the gift of a day. There's your one reason.

Live boldly and thrive.

The end!

Or, just the beginning...

KatrinaBusselle.com

Acknowledgments

This book would not exist without Kory Kirby and Fen Druadìn's inspired "Writing the Book Inside of You" workshop. Kory and Fen were my experienced guides, confidently showing me the way through the writing and publishing process. And look! Here we are at an end called "published."

A special shout-out to Dahlia Kaufman, my first reader and beloved friend, whose encouragement and feedback spurred me forward.

Max Traylor, thanks for inspiring me to be myself in book form and to do it my way.

Toward the end of the writing process, Kory informed me that I needed to give the book to three to five women I didn't know and ask for feedback and suggestions. He matter-of-factly said, "You can get the feedback now or when it's published, so let's get it now." This led me to Suzanne Banzer, Katie Franzen, Kate DiLeo, and Marnie Stockman. Even though we'd just met, they resoundingly said YES to my request to provide structured feedback on the project. Thank you!

And to William and Alexandra Busselle and Massimilliano Boccia. Thank you for allowing the chapters featuring your stories to be shared. I love you so much.

About the Author

Katrina Busselle is known for getting shit done. As an author, consultant, and coach, Katrina helps women live boldly and thrive. Over the course of her career, she has focused on leading teams to achieve big goals. She served as the director of community dispute resolution and the director of volunteers at Planned Parenthood, New York City, as director of marketing and communications and account management teams for a corporate wellness firm, and as a partner to a marketing agency specializing in B2B in the HR technology space. In partnership with Max Traylor, Katrina helps consultants productize, charge more, and put their personal lives first. She holds a bachelor's degree in psychology and mediation from Hampshire College, as well as a master of arts in conflict resolution from Antioch University. Katrina was born in New York City. When she was three, her family joined the Peace Corps and moved to West Africa, where she ran around in nothing but waist beads until she was six. After that, she spent most of her childhood in rural New York. Hated it. Found a home in Brooklyn in her mid-twenties. Loved it. Katrina relishes car conversations with her twins, hiking, finding presence on the yoga mat, jamming audiobooks and podcasts, and cooking with friends and family. She volunteers as a death doula for Hospice, helping people through the end of their natural lives. She currently resides in Cold Spring, New York. The daughter of Rebecca and Sam, Katrina is sister to two brothers, and partner to Massimilliano. She is a beloved friend to a handful of women who rock her world, and she is cherished by her community for her ability to listen, support, and advise on how to get shit done. Learn more about Katrina and her work at katrinabusselle.com.